—great thoughts on—

FAITH HOPE AND LOVE

COMPILED BY
CYNTHIA FRANKLIN AND TONI SORTOR

BARBOUR
PUBLISHING

—great thoughts on—

FAITH
HOPE AND
LOVE

Unless otherwise noted, all scripture quotations are taken from the HOLY BIBLE, NEW INTERNATIONAL VERSION®. NIV®. Copyright © 1973, 1978, 1984 by International Bible Society. Used by permission of Zondervan. All rights reserved.

Scripture quotations marked KJV are taken from the King James Version of the Bible.

Scripture quotations marked NKJV are taken from the New King James Version. Copyright © 1979, 1980, 1982 by Thomas Nelson, Inc. Used by permission. All rights reserved.

Scripture quotations marked NRSV are taken from the New Revised Standard Version Bible, copyright 1989, Division of Christian Education of the National Council of the Churches of Christ in the United States of America. Used by permission. All rights reserved.

Published by Barbour Publishing, Inc., P.O. Box 719, Uhrichsville, Ohio 44683 www.barbourbooks.com

Our mission is to publish and distribute inspirational products offering exceptional value and biblical encouragement to the masses.

Member of the
Evangelical Christian
Publishers Association

Printed in the United States of America.
5 4 3 2 1

CONTENTS

INTRODUCTION

And now these three remain:
faith, hope and love.
1 CORINTHIANS 13:13

What ingredients are essential for life? In the physical realm, human beings cannot live without food, water, and shelter. Spiritually speaking, those basic requirements are faith, hope, and love—the all-important trio the apostle Paul described in his first letter to the church in Corinth.

"Without faith it is impossible to please God, because anyone who comes to him must believe that he exists and that he rewards those who earnestly seek him," said the writer of the Bible's book of Hebrews. "In this hope we were saved," Paul wrote to Christians in Rome. "But the greatest of these is love," concludes 1 Corinthians 13:13, noted above.

Over the centuries, innumerable writers have celebrated the beauties of faith, hope, and love—whether in the ancient pages of scripture or in more recent prose and poetry. This small book, *Great Thoughts on Faith, Hope, and Love*, assembles several hundred quotations to encourage and inspire you. We hope that these collected truths will thrill your soul, lift your spirit, and fill your heart with gratitude to the God who provides "every good and perfect gift" (James 1:17).

THE EDITORS

FAITH

Faith is an action based upon a belief
that is supported by confidence.
R. W. SCHAMBACH

Belief is truth held in the mind;
faith is a fire in the heart.
JOSEPH FORT NEWTON

Some things have to be believed to be seen.
RALPH HODGSON

Belief is a moral act for which the
believer is to be held responsible.
H. A. HODGES

Talk unbelief, and you will have unbelief;
talk faith, and you will have faith.
According to the seed sown will be the harvest.
PLATO

The errors of faith are better than
the best thoughts of unbelief.
THOMAS RUSSELL

Be not faithless, but believing.
JOHN 20:27 KJV

Faith is the root of all blessings. Believe
and you shall be saved; believe and you
must needs be satisfied; believe and you
cannot but be comforted and happy.
JEREMY TAYLOR

FAITH

Faith is the father of all spiritual blessings.
UNKNOWN

The only faith that wears well and holds its color in all weathers, is that which is woven of conviction and set with the sharp mordant of experience.
JAMES RUSSELL LOWELL

A man of courage is also full of faith.
CICERO

Faith is putting all of your eggs into God's basket
and counting your blessings before they've hatched.
RAMONA C. CARROLL

Prefer a firm religious faith to every other blessing.
HUMPHREY DAVY

FAITH

The most valuable contribution a parent can make
to a child is to instill in him or her a genuine faith
in Jesus Christ.
JAMES C. DOBSON

Many of us have inherited great riches from our
parents; the bank account of personal faith and
family prayers.
NELS F. S. FERUE

Faith is the bird that sings while it is still dark.
PONSY

When you come to the edge of all the light you
know and are about ready to step off into the
darkness of the unknown, faith is knowing one of
two things will happen: there will be something
solid to stand on, or you will be taught how to fly.
BARBARA J. WINTER

Faith walks simply, childlike, between the darkness
of human life and the hope of what is to come.
CATHERINE DE HUECK DOHERTY

In this faith I wish to live and die.
FRANCOIS VILLON

Faith is the victory! Faith is the victory!
O glorious victory, that overcomes the world.
JOHN H. YATES

The faith in which we can live bravely
and die in peace must be certain.
JAMES A. FROUDE

"Though He slay me, yet will I trust Him"—
this is the most sublime utterance of faith
in the whole Bible.
OSWALD CHAMBERS

Feed your faith, and your
doubts will starve to death.
OUR DAILY BREAD

I show you doubt to prove that faith exists.
ROBERT BROWNING

Doubt your doubts, not your beliefs.
JO PETTY

Faith has no questions; doubt has no answers.
CLERGY TALK

Faith is two empty hands held open
to receive all of the Lord Jesus.
ALAN REDPATH

Faith is a certain image of eternity.
JEREMY TAYLOR

Never be afraid to trust an unknown
future to a known God
CORRIE TEN BOOM

I see heaven's glories shine, and faith shines equal,
arming me from fear.
EMILY BRONTE

Only believe, only believe;
All things are possible, only believe.
PAUL RADER

Every tomorrow has two handles. We can
take hold of it with the handle of
anxiety or the handle of faith.
HENRY WARD BEECHER

That is, that I may be comforted together with you
by the mutual faith both of you and me.
ROMANS 1:12 KJV

Faith expects from God what is
beyond all expectation.
ANDREW MURRAY

Faith makes the discords of the present
the harmonies of the future.
ROBERT COLLYER

Faith does nothing of itself but everything
under God, by God, and through God.
JOHN STOUGHTON

Faith that is sure of itself is not faith; faith that is
sure of God is the only faith there is.
OSWALD CHAMBERS

God hath dealt to every man the measure of faith.
ROMANS 12:3 KJV

It is not the greatness of faith that moves
mountains, but faith in the greatness of the Lord.
JO PETTY

FAITH

Seeds of faith are always with us; sometimes it takes
a crisis to nourish and encourage their growth.
SUSAN L. TAYLOR

Take the first step in faith. You don't have to see the
whole staircase—just take the first step.
MARTIN LUTHER KING JR.

Faith is building on what you know is here, so you
can reach what you know is there.
CULLEN HIGHTOWER

The secret behind getting more faith
is to get to know God more.
LESTER SUMERALL

Draw near with faith.
THE PRAYER BOOK

Faith is our spiritual oxygen. It not only keeps us
alive in God but enables us to grow stronger.
JOYCE LANDORF HEATHERLY

FAITH

The sweetest lesson I have learned in God's school
is to let the Lord choose for me.
DWIGHT L. MOODY

All the scholastic scaffolding fall, as a ruined edifice,
before one single word: faith.
NAPOLEON BONAPARTE

All I have seen teaches me to trust the Creator for
all I have not seen.
RALPH WALDO EMERSON

Understanding is the wage of a lively faith,
and faith is the reward of an humble ignorance.
FRANCIS QUARLES

A faith to live by, a self to live with,
and a purpose to live for. . .
BOB HARRINGTON

great thoughts on **FAITH, HOPE, AND LOVE**—31

FAITH

I am one of those who would rather
sink with faith than swim without it.
STANLEY BALDWIN

We must have faith, for this is the foundation;
we must have holiness of life,
for this is the superstructure.
CHARLES H. SPURGEON

Only let us persevere
Till we see our Lord appear,
Never from the Rock remove,
Saved by faith which works by love.
CHARLES WESLEY

The time demands strong minds,
great hearts, true faith.
JOSIAH GILBERT HOLLAND

FAITH

When reason is puzzling herself about a mystery,
faith is turning it into her daily bread
and feeding on it thankfully.
FREDERICK D. HUNTINGTON

Faith is not only a means of obeying,
but a principle act of obedience.
EDWARD YOUNG

As our faith increases, so does our ability to obey.
UNKNOWN

The principle part of faith is patience.
GEORGE MACDONALD

Faith is not worry or care,
but faith is fear that has said a prayer.
UNKNOWN

But I have prayed for thee, that thy faith fail not:
and when thou art converted,
strengthen thy brethren.
LUKE 22:32 KJV

Prayer and pains, through faith in Christ Jesus,
will do anything.
SIR JOHN ELIOT

I do not pray for success; I ask for faithfulness.
MOTHER TERESA

Faith, mighty faith, the promise sees and looks to
God alone, laughs at impossibilities and cries,
"It shall be done."
CHARLES WESLEY

By faith and faith alone, embrace,
believing where we cannot prove.
ALFRED, LORD TENNYSON

Faith is not belief without proof,
but trust without reservation.
ELTON TRUEBLOOD

If it can be verified, we don't need faith.
MADELEINE L'ENGLE

I need no other argument,
I need no other plea,
It is enough that Jesus died,
And that He died for me.
ELIZA E. HEWITT

Reason is an action of the mind;
knowledge is a possession of the mind;
but faith is an attitude of the person.
ARTHUR MICHAEL RAMSEY

Faith begins where reason sinks, exhausted.
ALBERT T. PIKE

Faith is believing in things when
common sense tells you not to.
GEORGE SEATON

Faith is a permanent and vital endowment
of the mind; a part of reason itself.
EDEN PHILLPOTTS

The soul of a civilization is its religion,
and it dies with its faith.
WILL AND ARIEL DURANT

I admire the serene assurance
of those who have religious faith.
MARK TWAIN

Welcome home again, discarded faith.
WILLIAM SHAKESPEARE

Let us have faith that right makes might.
ABRAHAM LINCOLN

This is faith: the renouncing of everything we are apt to call our own and relying wholly upon the blood, righteousness, and intercessions of Jesus.

JOHN NEWTON

For therein is the righteousness of God revealed from faith to faith: as it is written, The just shall live by faith.

ROMANS 1:17 KJV

Believing Christ died is history; believing Christ died for you is salvation.

OUR DAILY BREAD

My sin was old fashioned,
My guilt was old-fashioned,
God's love was old-fashioned, I know;
And the way I was saved was the old-fashioned way,
Through the blood that makes whiter than snow.
CIVILLA D. MARTIN

Faith is to believe on the Word of God,
what we do not see, and its reward is to
see and enjoy what we believe.
St. Augustine

I believe in Christianity as I believe in the sun;
not only because I see it, but because
by it I see everything else.
C. S. Lewis

My faith, it is an oaken staff,
The traveler's well loved aid;
My faith, it is a weapon stout,
The soldier's trusty blade.
THOMAS T. LYNCH

It is always right that a man should be able to render a reason for the faith that is within him.
SYDNEY SMITH

Little faith will bring your soul to heaven,
but great faith will bring heaven to your soul.
CHARLES H. SPURGEON

More strongly have faith and rejoice in Christ.
MARTIN LUTHER

Trials. . .are the very food of faith.
GEORGE MUELLER

God tries our faith so that
we may try His faithfulness.
UNKNOWN

We can go through anything if we
know that Jesus is going with us.
OUR DAILY BREAD

Leap, and the net will appear.
JULIE CAMERON

Faith involves letting go and
knowing God will catch you.
CLERGY TALK

Confirming the souls of the disciples,
and exhorting them to continue in the faith,
and that we must through much tribulation
enter into the kingdom of God.
ACTS 14:22 KJV

The steps of faith fall on the seeming
void but find the Rock beneath.
JOHN G. WHITTIER

If you know that God's hand is in everything,
you can leave everything in God's hand.
UNKNOWN

Faith is necessary to victory.
WILLIAM HAZLITT

Faith is not a sense, nor sight, nor reason,
but simply taking God at His word.
CHRISTMAS EVANS

He that is faithful in that which
is least is faithful also in much.
LUKE 16:10 KJV

Faith always has work to do.
CLERGY TALK

Trust God to move mountains but keep on digging.
OUR DAILY BREAD

Weave in faith, and God will find the thread.
PROVERB

FAITH

Faith and works are like the light and heat
of a candle; they cannot be separated.
JOSEPH BEAUMONT

Unless we do His teachings, we do not
demonstrate faith in Him.
EZRA TAFT BENSON

We must not sit still and look for miracles;
up and doing, and the Lord will be with thee.
FRANCIS DE SALES

God requires a faithful fulfillment of the merest trifle given us to do, rather than the most ardent aspiration to things to which we are not called.
FRANCES DE SALES

There shall never be an acceptable offering which has not been seasoned with faith
CHARLES H. SPURGEON

Faith is obedience at home and looking to the Master; obedience is faith going out to do His will.
ANDREW MURRAY

I have faith that yields to none.
OVID

There was never found in any age of the world that which did so highly exalt the public good as the Christian faith.
FRANCIS BACON

If we have received Christ in our innermost hearts, our new life will manifest its intimate acquaintance with Him by a walk of faith in Him.
CHARLES H. SPURGEON

Come to the clear flowing river,
Drink of its waters forever,
Hungry and thirsty, O! never,
Blessed are they that believe!
FANNY CROSBY

May the Christ in you be the hope
of glory to all who read.
BROTHER LAWRENCE

But as for me, I will always have hope;
I will praise you more and more.
PSALM 71:14 NIV

The joy of the LORD is your strength.
NEHEMIAH 8:10 NIV

Find rest, O my soul, in God alone;
my hope comes from him.
PSALM 62:5 NIV

There is no happiness which hope cannot
surmount, no grief which it cannot mitigate.
It is the wealth of the homeless, the health
of the sick, the freedom of the captive,
the rest of the laborer.
THEODORE LEDYARD CUYLER

O God, our help in ages past,
Our hope for years to come,
Our shelter from the stormy blast,
And our eternal home.
ISAAC WATTS

I press on toward the goal to win the
prize for which God has called me
heavenward in Christ Jesus.
PHILIPPIANS 3:14 NIV

Do not be anxious about anything, but in
everything, by prayer and petition, with
thanksgiving, present your requests to God.
PHILIPPIANS 4:6 NIV

Let us keep the hope of God in our
hearts and quiet in our minds.
BOLTON HALL

For hope to be real and genuine and not foolish or presumptuous, it must be grounded in God and God's promises.
ADAPTED FROM A NINETEENTH-CENTURY BIBLE DICTIONARY

We hope in Thee, O God!
The fading time is here,
But Thou abidest strong and true
Though all things disappear.
MARIANNE HEARN

Give me a faith that is without limit,
a hope that is ever unfailing,
and a love that is universal.
Francis of Assisi

Jesus! What a Friend for sinners!
Jesus! Lover of my soul;
Friends may fail me, foes assail me,
He, my Savior, makes me whole.
J. Wilbur Chapman

God is wise, and God is good. There is
nothing in the Bible that is not wise,
and there is nothing that is not good.
DWIGHT L. MOODY

Now faith is being sure of what we hope for
and certain of what we do not see.
HEBREWS 11:1 NIV

God has chosen to make known among the
Gentiles the glorious riches of this mystery,
which is Christ in you, the hope of glory.
COLOSSIANS 1:27 NIV

Christ in you is the one unanswerable evidence of
the ultimate victory.
G. CAMPBELL MORGAN

Hope is the gift of God's grace through
the blood of Jesus Christ, not a reward.
JOHN KNOX (ADAPTED)

"Because I live, you will live also." Believer,
read in these words of Jesus your glorious
title-deed. Your Savior lives—and His life
is the guarantee for your own life.
JOHN MACDUFF

Be strong and take heart,
all you who hope in the LORD.
PSALM 31:24 NIV

HOPE

Our hope is established in God's love—
God who gave us Christ as a pledge of His love.
This calls for us to return that love.

TERESA OF AVILA

I pray that out of his glorious riches he may
strengthen you with power through his Spirit
in your inner being, so that Christ may dwell
in your hearts through faith.

EPHESIANS 3:16–17 NIV

No one can lay a foundation other than the
one already laid, which is Jesus Christ.
1 CORINTHIANS 3:11 NIV

On Christ the solid Rock I stand;
All other ground is sinking sand,
All other ground is sinking sand.
EDWARD MOTE

HOPE

Cast all your anxiety on him
because he cares for you.
1 PETER 5:7 NIV

Give to the winds thy fears,
Hope, and be undismay'd;
God hears thy sighs and counts thy tears;
God shall lift up thy head.
PAULUS GERHARDT,
TRANSLATED BY JOHN WESLEY

HOPE

Looking for that blessed hope, and the
glorious appearing of the great God and
our Savior Jesus Christ.
TITUS 2:13 KJV

Take your stand on the Rock of Ages.
Let death, let the judgment come: The victory
is Christ's and yours through Him.
DWIGHT L. MOODY

Behold, all things are become new.
2 CORINTHIANS 5:17 KJV

Rest, and be still.
JEREMIAH 47:6 KJV

Now the man who is in Christ is the man who
has been born again, has become a partaker of the
Divine nature, and is indwelt by the Holy Spirit.
The person who is in Christ is justified before
God and freed from condemnation.
HARRY IRONSIDE

He is the Wonderful Counselor.
With tender sympathy, He can enter
into the innermost depths of your need.
JOHN MACDUFF

Be still, my soul: when change and fear are past,
All safe and blessed we shall meet at last.
KATHARINA VON SCHLEGEL,
TRANSLATED BY JANE BORTHWICK

He will wipe every tear from their eyes. There will
be no more death or mourning or crying or pain.
REVELATION 21:4 NIV

HOPE

The hope of every Christian is the place called
heaven—a better country. . . . They don't look
down to this earth, but they lift their eyes.
DWIGHT L. MOODY

To believe in hope, to have a full confidence
in that unseen power—this is the believing
which is acceptable to God.
JOHN WESLEY

Make an effort to find God in all. Disciplines
made part of the Christian life provide
hope in a believer's heart.
BENEDICT OF NURSIA

God does not give grace until the hour the trial
comes. . . . Tomorrow will bring its promised
grace along with tomorrow's trials.
JOHN MACDUFF

HOPE

"Whoever comes to me I will never drive away."
JOHN 6:37 NIV

Your sins are great, but your Savior's merits are
greater. He is willing to forget all the past and
sink it in oblivion, if there be present love
and the promise of future obedience.
JOHN MACDUFF

[God] according to his abundant mercy hath
begotten us again unto a lively hope by the
resurrection of Jesus Christ from the dead.
1 PETER 1:3 KJV

A lamp in the night, a song in time of sorrow;
A great glad hope which faith can ever borrow
To gild the passing day, with the glory of the morrow,
Is the hope of the coming of the Lord.
DANIEL W. WHITTLE

HOPE

Take it for granted upon the warrant of His word,
that you are His, and He is yours.
JOHN NEWTON

Some trust in chariots, and some in horses: but we
will remember the name of the LORD our God.
PSALM 20:7 KJV

I cannot understand how religious people
can remain content without the practice
of the presence of God.
BROTHER LAWRENCE

A man of many companions may come to ruin, but
there is a friend who sticks closer than a brother.
PROVERBS 18:24 NIV

Let the wicked forsake his way, and the
unrighteous man his thoughts: and let
him return unto the LORD, and he
will have mercy upon him.
ISAIAH 55:7 KJV

We will have confidence on the day of judgment,
because in this world we are like him.
1 JOHN 4:17 NIV

HOPE

Let nothing trouble you, let nothing make you afraid. All things pass away. God never changes. Patience obtains everything. God alone is enough.
TERESA OF AVILA

The duty required of us is to make the Lord our hope.
MATTHEW HENRY

To the King eternal, immortal, invisible, the only God, be honor and glory for ever and ever.
1 TIMOTHY 1:17 NIV

HOPE

"Come to me, all you who are weary and burdened,
and I will give you rest."
MATTHEW 11:28 NIV

Our chief fitness is in our utter helplessness.
His strength is made perfect, not in our strength,
but in our weakness.
HANNAH WHITALL SMITH

May he work in us what is pleasing to him, through
Jesus Christ, to whom be glory for ever and ever.
HEBREWS 13:21 NIV

In due season we shall reap, if we faint not.
GALATIANS 6:9 KJV

Believer! All the glory of your salvation belongs
to Jesus—none to yourself. Every jewel in your
eternal crown is His—purchased by His
blood and polished by His Spirit.
JOHN MACDUFF

HOPE

I saw one weary, sad, and torn,
With eager steps press on the way,
Who long the hallowed cross had borne,
Still looking for the promised day;
While many a line of grief and care,
Upon his brow, was furrowed there;
I asked what buoyed his spirits up,
"O this!" said he—"the blessed hope."

ANNIE R. SMITH

Only believe.
MARK 5:36 KJV

The briefest of the words of Jesus, but one
of the most comforting. They contain the
essence and epitome of all saving truth.
E. M. BOUNDS

Therefore, there is now no condemnation
for those who are in Christ Jesus.
ROMANS 8:1 NIV

I can speak from experience; I have been in
the Lord's service for twenty-one years,
and I want to testify that He is a good
paymaster—that He pays promptly.
DWIGHT L. MOODY

As far as the east is from the west, so far hath
he removed our transgressions from us.
PSALM 103:12 KJV

Why art thou so cast down, O my soul? and why
art thou disquieted in me? hope thou in God.
PSALM 42:5 KJV

The LORD will give grace and glory.
PSALM 84:11 KJV

"Having access by faith into this grace, you
can rejoice in hope of the glory of God," for
"whom he justifies, them he also glorifies."
JOHN MACDUFF

My hope and faith are firmly established in that promise—for now, as well as in the future.
DWIGHT L. MOODY

The LORD God is a sun and shield.
PSALM 84:11 KJV

We can rely only upon what Christ says, and He says, "He that believeth on me shall not perish, but have everlasting life."
DWIGHT L. MOODY

All my hope on God is founded;
He doth still my trust renew,
Me through change and chance He guideth,
Only good and only true.
JOACHIM NEANDER

"I am the gate; whoever enters through me
will be saved. He will come in and go out,
and find pasture."
JOHN 10:9 NIV

Christ's door is open to the poor—to any man,
whatever your life, whatever your character may be.
ROBERT MURRAY MCCHEYNE

HOPE

You will find him if you look for him with
all your heart and with all your soul.
DEUTERONOMY 4:29 NIV

The Holy Spirit speaking in the secret chambers
of the heart is the climax of God's revelation to us.
It is what gives us hope. None but God can satisfy
the longing of the immortal soul: The heart
was made for Him. He only can fill it.
RICHARD TRENCH

That He is merciful and just;
Here is my comfort and my trust.
MARTIN LUTHER

And thus my hope is in the Lord,
And not in my own merit;
I rest upon His faithful word
To them of contrite spirit.
MARTIN LUTHER

We know that in all things God works
for the good of those who love him.
ROMANS 8:28 NIV

The life of faith, then, consists in just this—being a
child in the Father's house. And when this is said,
enough is said to transform every weary, burdened
life into one of blessedness and rest.
HANNAH WHITALL SMITH

All suffering, sorrow, and loss are used by our
Father to minister to the benefit of believers.
A. W. PINK

Whispering hope, oh how welcome thy voice,
Making my heart in its sorrow rejoice.
SEPTIMUS WINNER

HOPE

Heaven is our home. We are longing for the great reunion with our beloved Lord, from whom we shall then never be separated.
CHARLES H. SPURGEON

As we are sanctified by faith, we must be sanctified by hope. So that we may be saved by hope, we must be purified by hope.
MATTHEW HENRY

Christ, of all my hopes the Ground;
Christ, the Spring of all my joy.
RALPH WARDLAW

O Christian, only believe that
there is a victorious life!
ANDREW MURRAY

Faith is the substance of things hoped for,
the evidence of things not seen.
HEBREWS 11:1 KJV

Faith and hope go together; and the same
things that are the object of our hope are the
object of our faith. It is a firm persuasion and
expectation that God will perform all that
He has promised to us in Christ.
MATTHEW HENRY

Who may ascend the hill of the LORD?
Who may stand in his holy place? He who
has clean hands and a pure heart.
PSALM 24:3–4 NIV

There can be no greater happiness than to place
one's all in Him who lacks nothing. Cast yourself,
all of yourself, with confidence into God and He
will sustain you, heal you, and make you safe.
ALBERT THE GREAT

In matters of religion, it is presumptuous
to hope that God's mercies will be poured
forth upon lazy persons who do nothing
toward holy and strict walking.
JEREMY TAYLOR

Let your hope be well-founded, according to
His revelation and promises. For it is possible
for a man to have a vain hope in God.
JEREMY TAYLOR

HOPE

You know you live in sin, yet you have a hope that
you shall be saved. . . . Why cleave to delusion and
death, when the truth is free, and eternal life in
Christ comes without money and without price?
CHARLES G. FINNEY

To one who is in great pain, God is the Physician
of body and of soul. I do not pray that you may
be delivered from your pains, but I pray to God
earnestly that He would give you strength and
patience to bear them as long as He pleases.
BROTHER LAWRENCE

HOPE

Jesus, my only Hope, be Thou my Guest;
Under Thy mighty wings, O let me rest,
Rest till the angel band home to the promised land
Bears me at Thy command, Savior, to Thee.
FANNY CROSBY

Light after darkness, gain after loss,
Strength after weakness, crown after cross.
FRANCES RIDLEY HAVERGAL

The days of your mourning shall be ended.
ISAIAH 60:20 NKJV

When the reaping time comes, the weeping
time ends. When the white robes and golden
harps are bestowed, every remnant of the
sackcloth attire is removed.
JOHN MACDUFF

God is enough! God is enough for time.
God is enough for eternity. *God is enough!*
HANNAH WHITALL SMITH

A musician is not commended for playing
long, but for playing well; it is obeying
God willingly that is accepted.
THOMAS WATSON

As we and you have one Lord, so we
have one Spirit: As we have one faith,
so we have one hope also.
JOHN WESLEY

Prisoners of hope, arise, and see your Lord appear;
Lo! on the wings of love He flies,
and brings redemption near.
CHARLES WESLEY

God does not want quick work, but good work.
God does not want slave work, but free work.
So, God is gentle with us all.
HENRY DRUMMOND

I need no other argument; I need no other plea.
It is enough that Jesus died, and that He died for me.
LIDIE H. EDMUNDS

It is by grace you have been saved, through faith—
and this not from yourselves, it is the gift of God—
not by works, so that no one can boast
EPHESIANS 2:8–9 NIV

Be of good courage. Will you not trust Him
to do this great work for you who has given
His life for you and has forgiven your sins?
ANDREW MURRAY

Rejoice, and be exceeding glad:
for great is your reward in heaven.
MATTHEW 5.12 KJV

Fear not; the God whom you serve is able to
deliver you; or, if he should suffer the flames to
devour your bodies, they would only serve, as so
many fiery chariots, to carry your souls to God.
GEORGE WHITEFIELD

HOPE

You ought to live holy and godly lives as you look forward to the day of God and speed its coming.
2 PETER 3:11–12 NIV

The most excellent method I have of going to God is in doing my common business without any view of pleasing men. My hope of glory is found in performing purely for the love of God.
BROTHER LAWRENCE

There is nothing like God-given hope to keep your mind fresh, provide you with a quicker step, offer you restful sleep at night, brighten your eyes, and put a smile on your face.
THOMAS BROOKS

It is hope that makes the soul exercise patience,
until the time comes to enjoy the crown.
JOHN BUNYAN

As a prisoner for the Lord, then, I urge you to live
a life worthy of the calling you have received.
EPHESIANS 4.1 NIV

Even if you have no other blessing on the
earth to call your own, you are rich indeed if
you can look up to heaven and say with a
smile, "I am at peace with God."
JOHN MACDUFF

Depth of mercy! Can there be
Mercy still reserved for me?
CHARLES WESLEY

My prayer for mercy was like the cry of ravens,
which yet the Lord does not disdain to hear. . .but
staked everything on the possibility of hope. I
sought mercy—and found it!
JOHN NEWTON

But lo! There breaks a yet more glorious day;
The saints triumphant rise in bright array;
The king of Glory passes on His way;
Alleluia, alleluia!
WILLIAM WALSHAM HOW

If human love is inexplicable, divine love is an ocean
too deep for the plummet of man or archangel,
too broad to be bounded by the thought of
the loftiest intelligence in the universe.
DANIEL STEELE

HOPE

The present time is most precious; now is the
accepted time, now is the day of salvation.
THOMAS A KEMPIS

Come, Thou long-expected Jesus,
Born to set Thy people free;
From our fears and sins release us,
Let us find our rest in Thee.
CHARLES WESLEY

We do not know Jesus until we love Him,
and the more we love, the more intimate
our knowledge of Him.
DANIEL STEELE

Our Lord Jesus Christ takes care to alter
and amend every prayer before He presents it,
and He makes the prayer perfect and
relevant with His own merits.
CHARLES H. SPURGEON

It is the right and portion of every believer to live
in the assurance that he is reconciled to God,
that God loves him, and that he is God's child.
If he does not live in that manner,
he has himself only to blame.
CHARLES H. SPURGEON

HOPE

My hope is built on nothing less
Than Jesus' blood and righteousness.
I dare not trust the sweetest frame,
But wholly trust in Jesus' Name.
EDWARD MOTE

I wish I could convince you that God is often (in some sense) nearer to us and more effectually present with us, in sickness than in health.
BROTHER LAWRENCE

He who knows himself the inheritor of all wealth and worlds and ages, yea, of power essential and in itself, that man has begun to be alive and, indeed, is full of hope.
GEORGE MACDONALD

HOPE

Faith is like love; it cannot be forced.
ARTHUR SCHOPENHAUER

Faith brings man to God; love brings Him to men.
MARTIN LUTHER

Faith is believing beyond the optic nerve.
UNKNOWN

Hope is the word God has written on the brow of
every man. Hope is the smile on God's face.
FROM NINETEENTH-CENTURY SERMONS

Christ's Resurrection is the groundwork
of our hope. And the new birth is our title
or evidence of our interest in it.
JOHN FLAVEL

Thank God for His Divine Providence in that He
has provided a way of escape from the road to hell.
SAMUEL RUTHERFORD

When the soul embraces itself, it sinks;
if it catches hold onto the power and promise
of God, it keeps the head above water.
MATTHEW HENRY

He hath put a new song in my mouth,
even praise unto our God.
PSALM 40:3 KJV

Those who wait for the LORD
shall renew their strength.
ISAIAH 40:31 NRSV

The scantiness or the fullness of your life all
depends upon how large a God you have!
A. B. SIMPSON

Sinners are prisoners, but they are prisoners of
hope: their case is sad, but it is not desperate.
MATTHEW HENRY

LOVE

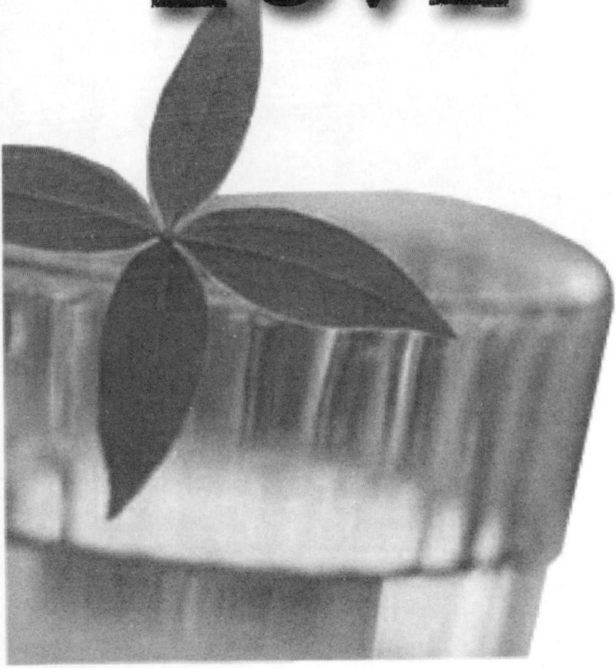

Choose your love, love your choice.
THOMAS S. MANSON

God is love, and to die means that I, a particle of
love, shall return to the general and eternal source.
LEO TOLSTOY

But as it is written, Eye hath not seen, nor ear
heard, neither have entered into the heart of
man, the things which God hath prepared
for them that love him.
1 CORINTHIANS 2:9 KJV

Familiar acts are beautiful through love.
PERCY BYSSHE SHELLY

Fate, time, occasion, chance, and change?
To these all things are subject but eternal love.
PERCY BYSSHE SHELLY

To be able to say how much you
love is to love but little.
PETRARCH

Bring love into your home, for this is
where our love for each other must start.
MOTHER TERESA

By this shall all men know that ye are my
disciples, if ye have love one to another.
JOHN 13:35 KJV

Brotherly love is still the distinguishing
badge of every true Christian.
MATTHEW HENRY

LOVE

There is no exception to God's
commandment to love everybody.
HENRY BUCKLEW

Be kindly affectioned one to another with brotherly
love; in honour preferring one another.
ROMANS 12:10 KJV

Love must be as much a light as it is a flame.
HENRY DAVID THOREAU

Love is an act of endless forgiveness,
a tender look which becomes a habit.
PETER USTINOV

People need loving the most
when they deserve it the least.
JOHN HARRIGAN

Freely we serve, because we freely love, as in
our will to love or not; in this we stand or fall.
JOHN MILTON

LOVE

Nothing we do, however virtuous, can be
accomplished alone; therefore, we are saved by love.
REINHOLD NIEBUHR

As long as we are loved by others, I would
say we are indispensable; no man is
useless while he has a friend.
ROBERT LOUIS STEVENSON

LOVE

No love, no friendship, can cross the path of our destiny without leaving some mark on it forever.
FRANCOIS MAURIAC

He who sows courtesy reaps friendship, and he who plants kindness gathers love.
ST. BASIL

A best friend is someone who loves you when you forget to love yourself.
UNKNOWN

LOVE

The love we give away is the only love we keep.
ELBERT HUBBARD

Love gives itself; it is not bought.
HENRY WADSWORTH LONGFELLOW

True love's the gift which God hath given
to man alone beneath the heaven.
WALTER DILL SCOTT

All love is sweet, given or returned.
PERCY BYSSHE SHELLEY

Every man is rich who has
a child to love and guide.
OUR DAILY BREAD

Love is the greatest thing that God can give us, for
He Himself is love; and it is the greatest thing we
can give to God, for it will also give ourselves.
JEREMY TAYLOR

LOVE

Always give people a little more love
and kindness than they deserve.
UNKNOWN

God gives us love; something to love He lends us.
ALFRED, LORD TENNYSON

The measure of God's love is that
he loves without measure.
ST. BERNARD

God must love the common man;
He made so many of them.
ABRAHAM LINCOLN

The God of love my Shepherd is.
GEORGE HERBERT

Beloved, let us love: for they who love,
They only, are His sons, born from above.
HORATIUS BONAR

LOVE

All loves should be simply stepping
stones to the love of God.
PLATO

Riches take wings, comforts vanish, hope withers
away, but love stays with us. God is love.
LEW WALLACE

Therefore thou shalt love the LORD thy God,
and keep his charge, and his statutes, and his
judgments, and his commandments, alway.
DEUTERONOMY 11:1 KJV

God loves us the way we are,
but too much to leave us that way.
UNKNOWN

Love is an image of God, and not a lifeless image,
but the living essence of the divine nature which
beams full of all goodness.
MARTIN LUTHER

LOVE

They say a person needs just three things to be truly happy in this world: someone to love, something to do, and something to hope for.
TOM BODETT

The supreme happiness of life is the conviction that we are loved, loved for ourselves, or rather loved in spite of ourselves.
VICTOR HUGO

Lonely hearts to comfort,
Weary lives to cheer—
This is our endeavor,
This our mission here;
Seeking out the lost ones
On the mountains cold,
We would gladly bring them
To the Shepherd's fold.

FANNY CROSBY

LOVE

One loving heart sets another on fire.
ST. AUGUSTINE

The heart that loves is always young.
GREEK PROVERB

Real love is helping someone
who can't return the favor.
UNKNOWN

Love is all we have, the only
way that each can help the other.
EURIPIDES

The heart of him who truly loves is a paradise on
earth; he has God in himself, for God is love.
ABBE HUGO DE LAMENNAIS

LOVE

Life with Christ is endless love;
without Him it is a loveless end.
BILLY GRAHAM

But God commendeth his love toward us, in that,
while we were yet sinners, Christ died for us.
ROMANS 5:8 KJV

Nails could not have kept Jesus on the
cross if love had not held Him there.
UNKNOWN

We love the Lord, of course, but we
often wonder what He finds in us.
EDGAR WATSON HOWE

If we love Christ much, surely
we shall trust Him much.
THOMAS BROOKS

Our Savior, Who is the Lord above all lords,
would have His servants known by
their badge, which is love.
HUGH LATIMER

LOVE

Life is short.
Be swift to love, make haste to be kind.
HENRI F. AMIEL

An ounce of love is worth a pound of knowledge.
JOHN WESLEY

The best portion of a good man's life is his little,
nameless, unremembered acts of kindness and love.
WILLIAM WORDSWORTH

Love is the hardest lesson in Christianity,
but for that reason, it should be the
most our care to learn it.
WILLIAM PENN

Father, make us loving, gentle, thoughtful, kind;
Fill us with Thy Spirit, make us of Thy mind.
Help us love each other, more and more each day,
Help us follow Jesus, in the narrow way.
FLORA KIRKLAND

We are not made for law, but for love.
GEORGE MACDONALD

I love these little ones, and it is not a slight thing
when they, who are so fresh from God, love us.
CHARLES DICKENS

And to know the love of Christ, which
passeth knowledge, that ye might be
filled with all the fulness of God.
EPHESIANS 3:19 KJV

We are shaped and fashioned by what we love.
JOHANN WOLFGANG VON GOETHE

To have and be loved is to feel
the sun from both sides.
DAVID VISCOTT

What most people need to learn in life is
how to love people and use things instead
of using people and loving things.
UNKNOWN

LOVE

Love and a cough cannot be hid.
GEORGE HERBERT

To love for the sake of being loved is human,
but to love for the sake of loving is angelic.
ALPHONSE DE LAMATINE

Love begets love.
THEODORE ROETHKE

Love is love's reward.
JOHN DRYDEN

If you would be loved, love and be lovable.
BENJAMIN FRANKLIN

If there is anything better than
to be loved, it is to love.
UNKNOWN

LOVE

Do you know the world is dying
For a little bit of love?
Everywhere we hear the sighing
For a little bit of love;
For the love that rights a wrong,
Fills the heart with hope and song;
They have waited, oh, so long,
For a little bit of love.
EDWIN O. EXCELL

It may be risky to marry for love, but it's so honest that the Lord just has to smile on it.
JOSH BILLINGS

The first duty of love is to listen.
PAUL TILLICH

No cord or cable can draw so forcibly, or bind so fast, as love can do with a single thread.
RICHARD E. BURTON

Husbands, love your wives, even as Christ
also loved the church, and gave himself for it.
EPHESIANS 5:25 KJV

Love does not consist of gazing at each other
but in looking together in the same direction.
ANTOINE DE SAINTE-EXUPERY

Love is like a pair of socks; you gotta
have two and they gotta match.
UNKNOWN

Immature love says, "I love you because I need you."
Mature love says, "I need you because I love you."
ERICH FROMM

It is a beautiful necessity of
our nature to love something.
DOUGLAS JERROLD

I have found the paradox that if I love until it
hurts, then there is no hurt but only more love.
MOTHER TERESA

LOVE

Songbirds in the woodlands sing it,
Flowers breathe it in the grove,
Bells in tow'r and steeple ring it—
God is goodness, God is love.
JAMES ROWE

Love is the great miracle cure.
LOUISE HAY

A good father reflects the
love of the heavenly Father.
UNKNOWN

One word frees us of all the weight
and pain of life. That word is love.
SOPHOCLES

Who, being loved, is poor?
OSCAR WILDE

Love is infallible; it has no errors,
for all the errors are the want of love.
WILLIAM LAW

It is astonishing how little one
feels poverty when one loves.
EDWARD BULWER-LYTTON

Holding the heart of another in the comforting
hands of prayer is a priceless act of love.
JANET L. WEAVER

They do not love that do not show their love.
WILLIAM SHAKESPEARE

Love is shown in your deeds, not in your words.
JEROME CUMMINGS

LOVE

Love looks not with the eyes but with the mind.
WILLIAM SHAKESPEARE

Blessed is the influence of one
true, loving soul on another.
GEORGE ELIOT

Joy is the net of love by which you can catch souls.
MOTHER TERESA

O praise our God today,
His constant mercy bless,
Whose love hath helped us on our way,
And granted us success.
HENRY W. BAKER

Treasure the love you receive above all.
It will survive long after your gold
and good health have vanished.
OG MAGDINO

But if any man love God,
the same is known of him.
1 CORINTHIANS 8:3 KJV

Many people mistake our work for our vocation.
Our vocation is the love of Jesus.
MOTHER TERESA

And I have declared unto them thy name, and will
declare it: that the love wherewith thou hast loved
me may be in them, and I in them.
JOHN 17:26 KJV

Love is to the mortal nature
what the sun is to the earth.
HONORE DE BALZAC

Take away love, and our earth is a tomb.
ROBERT BROWNING

When love and skill work
together, expect a masterpiece.
JOHN RUSKIN

LOVE

The love of God is greater far
Than tongue or pen can ever tell;
It goes beyond the highest star,
And reaches to the lowest hell;
The guilty pair, bowed down with care,
God gave His Son to win;
His erring child He reconciled,
And pardoned from his sin.

FREDERICK M. LEHMAN

Never forget that the most
powerful force on earth is love.
NELSON ROCKEFELLER

Love doesn't make the world go around;
love is what makes the ride worthwhile.
FRANKLIN P. JONES

Love is the river of life in the world.
HENRY WARD BEECHER

LOVE

For God so loved the world, that he gave his only
begotten Son, that whosoever believeth in him
should not perish, but have everlasting life.

JOHN 3:16 KJV

Jesus answered and said unto him, If a man love
me, he will keep my words: and my Father will
love him, and we will come unto him,
and make our abode with him.

JOHN 14:23 KJV

LOVE

Wide, wide as the ocean,
high as the Heaven above;
Deep, deep as the deepest sea
is my Savior's love.
I, though so unworthy,
still am a child of His care;
For His Word teaches me
that His love reaches me everywhere.
C. AUSTIN MILES

LOVE

Love one another, and you will be happy.
It's as simple and as difficult as that.
MICHAEL LEUNIG

Love seeks to make happy rather than to be happy.
RALPH CONNOR

Beloved, let us love one another: for love
is of God; and every one that loveth
is born of God, and knoweth God.
1 JOHN 4:7 KJV

Joy is love aware of its own inner happiness.
FULTON J. SHEEN

Love is the master key which
opens the gates of happiness.
OLIVER WENDELL HOLMES

Happiness is the spiritual experience of living
every minute with love, grace, and gratitude.
DENIS WAITLEY

LOVE

Love has always been the most
important business of my life.
HENRI BEYLE

We'll go, like the Savior, to comfort the sad;
With love's healing portion we'll make others glad,
Until, with fresh verdure, life's deserts are clad;
Somebody else needs a blessing.
ELIZA E. HEWITT

Life is a flower of which love is the honey.
VICTOR HUGO

You will find, as you look back on your life, that
the moments when you have really lived are the
moments you have done things in the spirit of love.
HENRY DRUMMOND

LOVE

Immortal love, forever full,
Forever flowing free,
Forever shared, forever whole,
A never ebbing sea!

O Lord and Master of us all,
Whate'er our name or sign,
We own Thy sway, we hear Thy call,
We test our lives by Thine.
JOHN G. WHITTIER

Love comforteth like sunshine after rain.
WILLIAM SHAKESPEARE

Not father or mother has loved you as
God has, for it was that you might
be happy He gave His only Son.
HENRY WADSWORTH LONGFELLOW

Don't hold to anger, hurt, or pain; they
steal your energy and keep you from love.
LEO F. BUSCAGLIA

Love is the golden chain that binds
The happy souls above;
And he's an heir of Heaven who finds
His bosom glow with love.
JOSEPH SWAIN

For whom the LORD loveth he correcteth; even
as a father the son in whom he delighteth.
PROVERBS 3:12 KJV

The Master, who loved most of all, endured the
most and proved His love by His endurance.
HUGH B. BROWN

Love is not blind; it sees more, not less, but
because it sees more, it chooses to see less.
UNKNOWN

LOVE

So ought men to love their wives as their own
bodies. He that loveth his wife loveth himself.
EPHESIANS 5:28 KJV

Down on your knees, and thank heaven,
fasting, for a good man's love.
WILLIAM SHAKESPEARE

The most important thing a father can do
for his children is to love their mother.
THEODORE HESBURGH

I like not only to be loved, but
also to be told that I am loved.
GEORGE ELIOT

Tell someone you love them. Tell them again.
UNKNOWN

The desire to be beloved is ever restless and
unsatisfied, but the love that flows out upon
others is a perpetual wellspring from on high.
LYDIA M. CHILD

LOVE

Love is the circle that doth restless
move in the same sweet eternity of love.
ROBERT HERRICK

Love is the lesson which the Lord us taught.
EDMUND SPENCER

God gave us free choice because there is no significance in love that knows no alternative.
BREAD OF LIFE

Jesus said unto him, Thou shalt love the Lord thy God with all thy heart, and with all thy soul, and with all thy mind.
MATTHEW 22:37 KJV

LOVE

Write down the advice of him who loves
you though you like it not at the present.
SPANISH PROVERB

It is your unlimited power to care
and to love that can make the biggest
difference in the quality of your life.
ANTHONY ROBBINS

One may give without loving, but
one cannot love without giving.
UNKNOWN

Love has nothing to do with what you
are expecting to get; it's what you are
expecting to give—which is everything.
KATHERINE HEPBURN

I am persuaded, that neither death,
nor life, nor angels, nor principalities,
nor powers, nor things present, nor things
to come, nor height, nor depth, nor any other
creature, shall be able to separate us from the
love of God, which is in Christ Jesus our Lord.
ROMANS 8:38–39 KJV

LOVE

Between whom there is hearty truth, there is love.
HENRY DAVID THOREAU

The heart that has truly loved never forgets.
THOMAS MOORE

To love is to place our happiness
in the happiness of another.
BARON GOTTFRIED WILHELM VON LEIBNITZ

Behold th'amazing gift of love
The Father hath bestowed
On us, the sinful sons of men,
To call us sons of God!
ISAAC WATTS

Behold, what manner of love the
Father hath bestowed upon us, that
we should be called the sons of God.
1 JOHN 3:1 KJV

We can't form our children on
our own concepts; we must take them
and love them as God gives them to us.
JOHANN WOLFGANG VON GOETHE

The God who made your children
will hear your petitions. After all,
He loves them more than you do.
JAMES DOBSON

God loved the world so that He gave
His only Son the lost to save
That all who would in Him believe
Should everlasting life receive.
AUTHOR UNKNOWN,
TRANSLATED BY AUGUST KRULL.

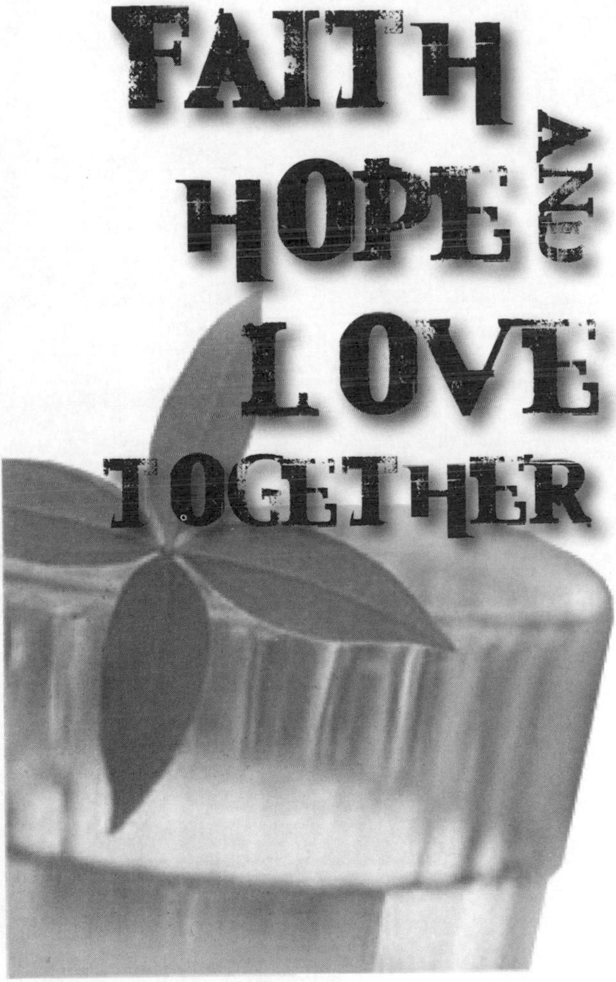
FAITH
HOPE AND
LOVE
TOGETHER

Faith and hope go together; and the
same things that are the object of our
hope are the object of our faith.
MATTHEW HENRY

Grant me, good Lord, a full faith, a firm hope,
and a fervent love, that I may desire only that
which gives You pleasure and conforms to Your favor.
THOMAS MORE

When you put faith, hope, and love together, you
can raise positive kids in a negative world.
ZIG ZIGLAR

Hope is like a harebell, trembling from its birth,
Love is like a rose, the joy of all the earth,
Faith is like a lily, lifted high and white,
Love is like a lovely rose, the world's delight.
Harebells and sweet lilies show a thornless growth,
But the rose with all its thorns excels them both.
CHRISTINA ROSSETTI

Let Christian faith and hope dispel
The fears of guilt and woe;
The Lord Almighty is our Friend,
And who can prove a foe?
JOHN LOGAN

To be of no church is dangerous. Religion,
of which the rewards are distant, and which
is animated only by faith and hope, will glide
by degrees out of the mind unless it be invig-
orated and reimpressed by external ordinances,
by stated calls to worship, and the salutary
influence of example.
SAMUEL JOHNSON

So long as faith with freedom reigns
And loyal hope survives,
And gracious charity remains
To leaven lowly lives;
While there is one untrodden tract
For intellect or will,
And men are free to think and act,
Life is worth living still.
ALFRED AUSTIN

Fear forces, love leads, faith follows.
KEITH MOORE

In faith and hope the world will disagree,
But all mankind's concern is charity.
ALEXANDER POPE

Faith will vanish into sight;
Hope be emptied in delight;
Love in heaven will shine more bright;
Therefore, give us Love.

Faith and Hope and Love we see
Joining hand in hand agree;
But the greatest of the three,
And the best, is Love.
CHRISTOPHER WORDSWORTH

Lord, dismiss us with thy blessing,
Hope, and comfort from above;
Let us each, thy peace possessing,
Triumph in redeeming love.
ROBERT HAWKER

Inspirational Library

Beautiful purse/pocket-sized editions of Christian classics bound in flexible leatherette. These books make thoughtful gifts for everyone on your list, including yourself!

When I'm on My Knees　　　The highly popular collection of devotional thoughts on prayer, especially for women.
　　　Flexible Leatherette. $4.97

The Bible Promise Book　　　Over 1,000 promises from God's Word arranged by topic. What does God promise about matters like: Anger, Illness, Jealousy, Love, Money, Old Age, and Mercy? Find out in this book!
　　　Flexible Leatherette. $3.97

Daily Wisdom for Women　　　A daily devotional for women seeking biblical wisdom to apply to their lives. Scripture taken from the New American Standard Version of the Bible.
　　　Flexible Leatherette. $5.97

A Gentle Spirit　　　With an emphasis on personal spiritual development, this daily devotional for women draws from the best writings of Christian female authors.
　　　Flexible Leatherette. $5.97

Available wherever books are sold.
Or order from:

Barbour Publishing, Inc.
P.O. Box 719
Uhrichsville, OH 44683
www.barbourbooks.com

If you order by mail, add $2.00 to your order for shipping.
Prices are subject to change without notice.